How to make
MOBILES

To my children and grandchildren,
with love.

How to make
MOBILES

Polly Pinder

SEARCH PRESS

First published in Great Britain 1997

Search Press Limited
Wellwood, North Farm Road,
Tunbridge Wells, Kent TN2 3DR

ISBN 0 85532 814 2

*The author would like to thank Winsor and Newton
for providing their Galeria range of acrylic paints
which have been an invaluable asset in the
completion of models for this book.*

Printed in Spain by Elkar S Coop, Bilbao 48012

Contents

Introduction

Making things is such a wonderful antidote to stress and melancholy, I am surprised it is not prescribed as a valid alternative to medicine. One is completely absorbed, fascinated, in a small, comfortable world which is creative, positive and deeply satisfying. The real joy and healing power of simple creativity should not be over-estimated. Of course there are the occasional hitches – the collapse of an object on which hours of work have been lavished is no laughing matter; and the piece that refuses to stick, even if it were spot welded, causes concern. The waste bin may contain a collection of 'first attempts', but a quiet faith pushes us onward and sometimes the final result can be breathtaking. But, no matter what, it at least provides a lovely sense of achievement.

Mobiles are fun, they add a bright splash of moving colour – a jolly statement. They are mainly light-hearted but they can also be stunningly beautiful.

I have divided this book into two sections. The first involves mobiles made from lots of different materials, many of which you may already have in the kitchen, in the cupboard under the stairs, or in the garden shed. The second part relies on nature to provide the basics – leaves, petals, seeds, evergreen foliage and other delights. All the projects are described in detailed stages but they need not be followed religiously. The ideas and techniques can be used as a springboard for further development. You may be familiar with some methods; others will be quite new, but whether you are following the instructions to the letter or improvising, always aim for a professional finish, believing that 'handmade' should imply care, skill and attention to detail.

Mobiles make wonderful gifts. The objects, colours, textures and basic construction are so variable that any mood can be achieved, any diverse personality catered for. I still believe, after many years' involvement and seeing the amazing displays of gifts now available, that something well made with love, will be treasured more highly than any number of expensive presents.

Creating
colourful mobiles

METAL COASTERS • GLASS PAINTING • FEATHERS AND CORKS

SALT DOUGH • FABRIC FISH • CARD AND CLAY

PAPIER MÂCHÉ

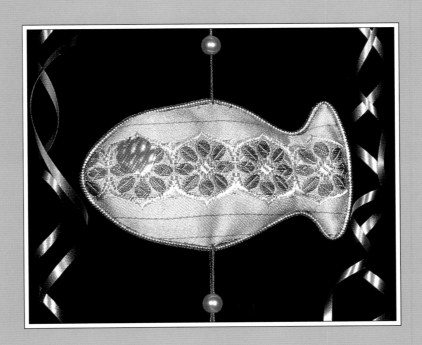

Coaster chimes

Little metal coasters were being sold very cheaply at our local market and I thought they would make an ideal mobile – something bright and shiny to catch the light. The slightest breeze sends them spinning and, being just close enough to touch, they give a pleasant short-lived ring. The letters, which read GO TO SLEEP, were drawn with the aid of a plastic stencil then hand painted. Alternatively you could use dry transfer letters (available from most art and craft shops).

Tools and materials

6mm (¼in) square beading: two 400mm (16in) and one 10mm (³⁄₈in) lengths.

Wood glue, PVA, impact adhesive and double-sided sticky tape.

Large bead, brass ring, nine very small eye screws and one larger one

Gold spray paint (ozone friendly), white poster paint, blue permanent marker pen

Metal coasters (eighteen)

Holographic wrapping paper, thin metallic card

Scissors, pencil and compass, bradawl and pliers

Plastic letter stencil or dry transfer letters

Gold sewing thread, thick and fine

1 Using wood glue, stick the two long lengths of beading together at right angles and then stick the small length over the join to make the support.

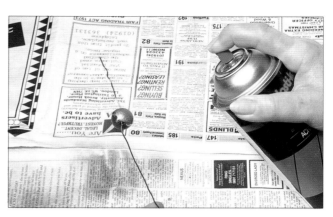

2 Spray the support, both sides of each coaster and the large bead (threaded on a length of wire) with gold paint.

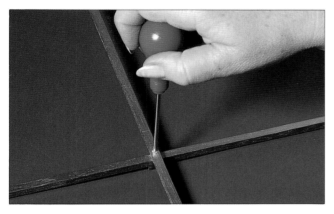

3 Using a bradawl, make small holes in the centre of the top beading, the centre of the small piece underneath and at intervals of 75mm (3in) along the underside of the four prongs.

4 Screw the larger eye screw into the top hole and the small ones in the other holes.

5 Cut the fine gold thread into one 250mm (10in), four 330mm (13in) and four 400mm (16in) lengths. Fold them in half and stick to the back of nine coasters with double-sided tape.

6 Arrange the coasters in pairs (one with the thread attached, one without). Spread a thin film of impact adhesive on to the backs of each pair then stick them together.

7 Measure the inner diameter of a coaster then carefully cut out circles of holographic paper. Stick them to each side of the coasters with PVA.

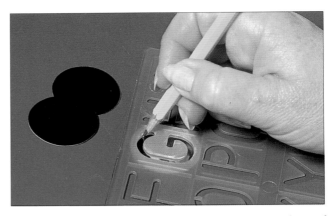

8 Cut nine 38mm (1½in) diameter circles of metallic card. Using the stencil and a blunt pencil draw the letters G, O, T, O, S, L, E, E, P on each one.

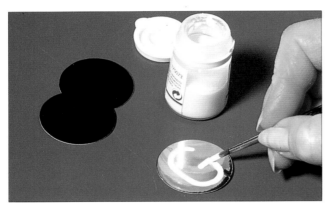

9 Using white poster paint, fill in the letters. Use PVA to stick a disc in the centre of one side of each pair of coasters.

10 Using a permanent marker pen, draw a simple dancing figure on the other side of each coaster.

11 Pass a 380mm (15in) length of thick gold thread through the brass ring, the bead, the large eye screw, back through the bead and tie a knot. Place the knot in the middle of the thread and cover with the bead.

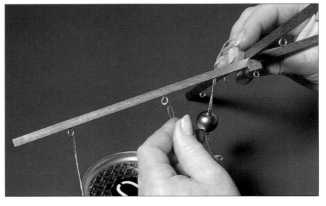

12 Attach the coasters to the eye screws. The join of each eye should be wide enough to slip the fine gold thread through – if it is not, open it slightly with a pair of pliers.

Stained-glass windows

This imitation stained-glass mobile was made to hang against, or just in front of, a large window. Pieces of clear acetate were painted with glass paint and framed with black card. The paint is available at most hobby/craft shops together with tubes of relief outliner. I find outliner awkward to use, so I make my own and apply it through an icing nozzle. Any simple design can be used for the little windows; geometric, floral, animals etc. Tiny black glass beads threaded on to black cotton were used to hang the windows, but fine chain or embroidery silk could be used instead.

Tools and materials

Simple outline designs

A4 sheets of clear acetate

Glass paints, solvent and a paint brush

Relief outliner or home-made leading (see below)

Black mounting board, white conté crayon or chalk

Scissors, a craft knife and a steel-edged ruler

Circle cutter (for round designs), cutting mat or thick cardboard

Double-sided sticky tape and masking tape

Black felt-tipped pen and a pencil

Darning needle, fine sewing needle, some black cotton thread and some tiny black glass beads

Small hammer

Home-made leading

For home-made leading you need:

5 heaped teaspoons plain flour

5 teaspoons of water

2 heaped teaspoons of PVA

Small blob of black food colour

Greaseproof paper, No.1 icing nozzle, small bowl, a mixing spoon and plastic kitchen wrap

1. Blend the flour and water together and then add the PVA and food colour. Mix until perfectly smooth, adding more flour if the mixture is too runny or PVA if it is too stiff. Cover the surface of the mixture with plastic kitchen wrap and smooth it down to expel all air.

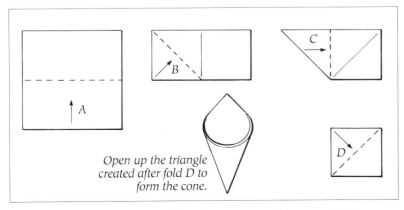

Open up the triangle created after fold D to form the cone.

2. Cut a 250mm (10in) square from the greaseproof paper and fold as shown to form a cone.

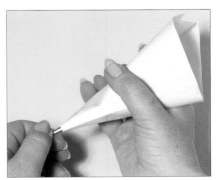

3. Snip the end off the point of the cone, drop in the icing nozzle and pull it down tightly. Add a few spoonfuls of mixture when you are ready to pipe.

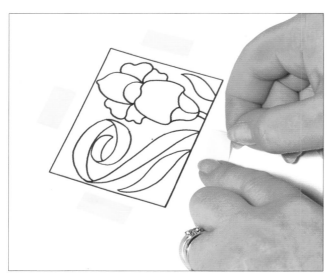

1 Cut a piece of acetate large enough to overlap your chosen design and attach it to the design with masking tape.

2 Using relief outliner or your own mixture, draw the leading on to the acetate following the lines of the design. Do not draw the perimeter lines of the design as these will be covered by the frame. Leave the leading to dry for an hour.

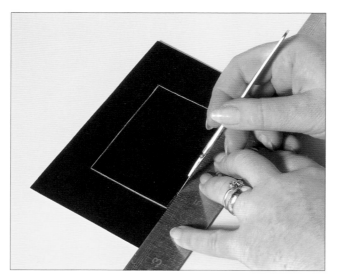

3 Each little design must be sandwiched between two identical frames. For rectangular and square frames cut two pieces of card about 25mm (1in) larger all round than the design. Using white chalk or conté crayon draw the outline on to each then, using the craft knife and steel-edged ruler, cut out the centre. These shapes can be trimmed to a final size after the painted acetate has been sandwiched between the two card frames.

4 Circular frames must be cut to the final size (using a circle cutter) before the acetate is framed. For this example I used a 12mm (½in) border and cut the outside of the circle first.

5 Blacken the cut edges with the felt-tipped pen. Turn the piece over and, just in case the two cut-outs aren't perfectly matched, blacken round the inside edge of the frame.

6 Put the frames to one side and start colouring the design. Slightly flood each section so that no brush strokes are visible. Paint beyond the perimeter lines in case the inside of the frame is a little too large. The colours can be mixed. Leave to dry for thirty minutes.

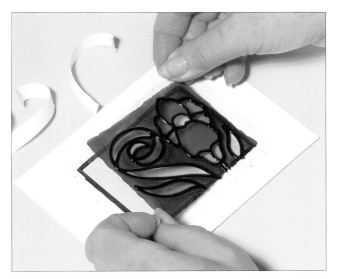

7 Attach strips of double-sided sticky tape to the white sides of both sections of the frame and carefully press the design on to one of them.

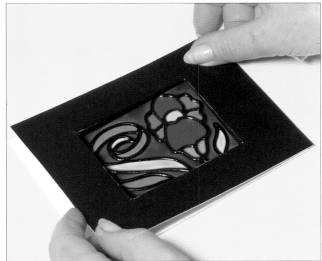

8 Attach the other frame making sure that it lines up all round. If necessary, trim the frame to the correct size and blacken the edges.

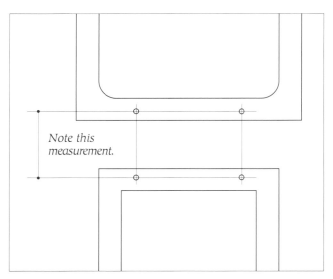

9 When all the designs have been framed, arrange them in the position in which you want them to hang. Measure and make a note of the distance between each. Mark with a pencil the positions of holes in each frame.

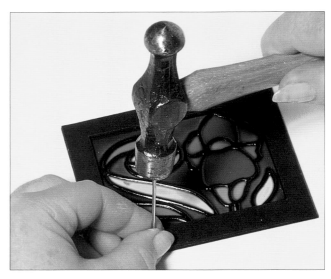

10 Pierce the holes by pushing a darning needle through with the aid of a couple of taps from the hammer.

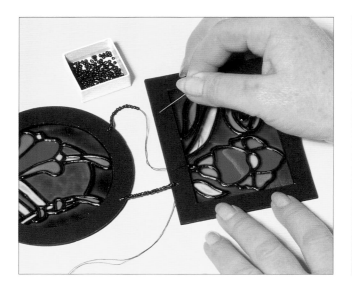

11 Thread the sewing needle and push it up through one of the holes. Thread some beads, referring to the measurements on your diagram, then push the needle down through the corresponding hole in the other frame. Repeat with the second hole in each of the two frames.

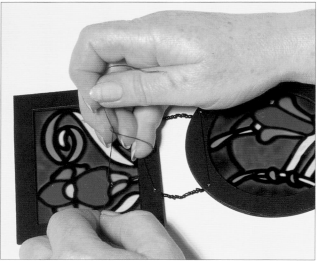

12 Turn the pieces over and tie the loose threads together using two knots; secure with a dab of PVA. Continue until all the windows are joined.

Stained-glass window mobile

Stick the completed mobile to a window using neat pieces of double-sided sticky tape. Alternatively, screw the design to the window frame or hang it in front of a window, suspended on a thin pole supported by a couple of hooks.

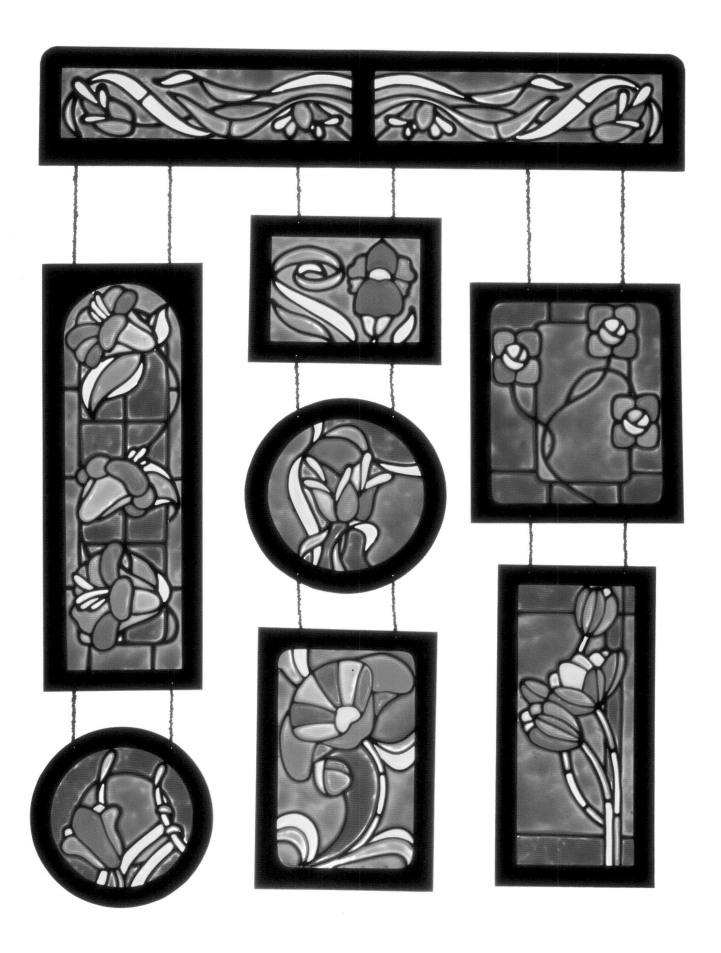

Spiralling birds

The delicate nature of a feather is so appealing. Seen against the light it becomes magical – then a single breath of air brings silent, effortless movement. Young children will be fascinated as they watch these little floating birds and nod off to sleep.

The colour scheme will depend on the available range of feathers. I mixed my paints for the birds' bodies and beaks to match the feathers then bought the modelling clay, which has an extensive range, to match the spray paint for the nest. Softer or brighter colours can be used.

Tools and materials

Tapered bottle corks (twelve) available from home-brew stores

Darning/tapestry needle

Modelling clay which is hardened in the oven (available from most craft shops)

Coloured feathers (available from most craft shops)

Spray paint (ozone friendly), acrylic paints to match the feathers and a paint brush

PVA and sticky tape

Beads: six small glass beads to use as weights and twenty-four tiny, shiny beads to use as eyes

Tweezers

Scissors

Pencil and compass

Invisible, plastic thread and small metal ring

White card roughly 150mm (6in) square

Wreath frame approximately 150mm (6in) diameter (available from florists or craft shops).

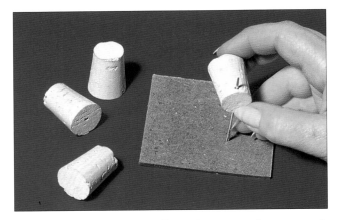

1 Using a darning needle and a piece of scrap card, pierce a hole through the narrow end of each cork. Ensure the hole is clear.

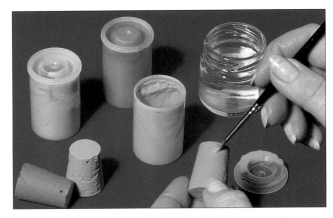

2 Paint the corks – paint the top half first, leave it to dry then turn it over and paint the bottom half. Two coats will be needed to get a good colour.

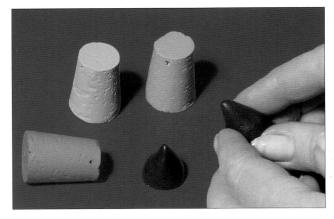

3 Shape the clay to fit the tapered end of the cork and form a conical head. Harden in the oven (read the manufacturer's instructions).

4 When the clay has cooled, paint beaks on to the pointed ends of each head and then attach them to the corks with PVA.

5 Make a hole in the wide end of each cork and push a feather into the hole to make a tail.

6 Trim the tips from some feathers for wings. Attach to the sides of each cork with PVA.

7 Place some PVA in a saucer. Using the tweezers carefully dip each tiny bead into the glue then position on each bird's head.

8 Spray the wreath frame and one side of the card.

9 Push any remaining feather pieces into the frame.

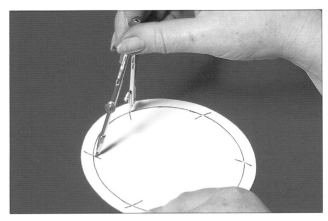

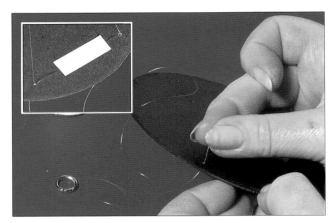

10 Cut a 125mm (5in) diameter card disc (or one 25mm (1in) smaller than the wreath). Draw a circle inside leaving a 10mm (³/₈in) border, then use the compass to divide the circle into six.

11 Pierce the marks with a darning needle. Spray the circle to cover all the pencil marks. Cut three 560mm (22in) lengths of invisible thread. Thread one through the metal ring, down through one hole in the circle of card and up through the next one. Tie the ends together and position the knot so that it rests on top of the card. Repeat with the other two lengths.

Cut three more lengths of thread, 1.25m (50in) long, and pass the ends of each piece down through two adjacent holes. Make all ends the same length and fix in place with a small piece of sticky tape across the top of the card.

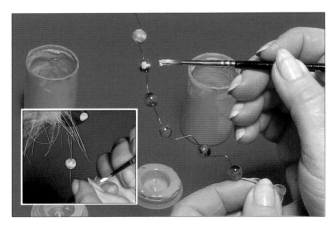

12 Now thread on the birds – push the thread down through the hole at the head, take it up round one side, down through the hole again, up round the other side and down through the hole. Work round the mobile placing each bird slightly lower than the previous one. Continue until each thread carries two birds.

13 Thread the glass beads on to a length of thin wire and paint them with blobs of the four colours used for the corks. Attach the bead to the ends of each thread using the same triple method as for the corks. Dab a tiny streak of PVA on to the very end of the thread to secure.

14 Complete the mobile by sliding the nest on to the cardboard circle.

Spiralling birds

The finished mobile. A more natural scheme would be achieved by leaving the corks and wreath frame as they are, perhaps threading dried leaves and berries through the frame and using a more subtle selection of undyed feathers.

Salt dough shapes

The shapes and ring for this simple mobile are made from salt dough (flour, water and salt). Children can assist at most stages of the process – rolling and cutting the dough, painting the shapes when they have cooled, then threading the shapes and beads in preparation for hanging.

Tools and materials

1 mug plain flour, ½ mug fine household salt and 250ml (9 fl oz) warm water

Basin, rolling pin and two 6mm (¼in) thick strips of wood, saucer, plain ring pastry cutter, some small cocktail cutters and some wooden cocktail sticks

Baking tray or flat microwave-proof plate

Brightly coloured acrylic paint, water-based clear satin varnish and a paint brush

Fifty-six matching coloured wooden beads and a plastic or metal ring for hanging

Embroidery silk or wool

Darning needle, scissors

PVA glue

Making salt dough

To make sufficient salt dough for this mobile, mix one mug of flour with half a mug of salt and then slowly add enough water to make a clean dough – not wet enough to be sticky nor dry enough to be crumbly. The dough will keep for about two days in the fridge. Work the dough and cut out the shapes as shown.

Salt dough shapes can be baked in an oven or microwave. Cooking times will vary: as a rough guide, bake for three to four hours in an oven at gas mark 2 or 300°F (150°C), or for about twenty minutes in a microwave on the low or warm setting. Experiment with one or two pieces before baking all the shapes. The dough will be baked when the surface looks dry and it sounds hollow when tapped.

To be able to thread the shapes you will need to make holes in them when they are firm enough to handle but still soft in the middle – after thirty minutes in the oven or four minutes in the microwave.

1. Knead the dough on a lightly floured surface until it becomes smooth, malleable and elastic.

2. Using the wooden sticks as a thickness guide, roll out the pastry to an even thickness.

3. Cut about forty different shapes (only thirty six are needed but it's always useful to have a few extra).

4. Make the hanging ring using a saucer for the outer circle and a plain cutter for the core.

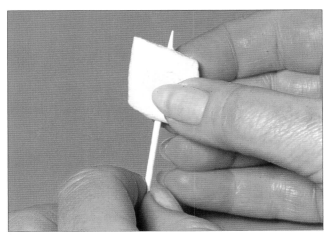

1 Place all the shapes on a baking tray and place in a preheated oven for about thirty minutes, or place them on a microwave-proof plate and cook for four minutes in a microwave.

2 Remove the tray; the shapes should be firm but still soft. Using wooden cocktail sticks, make a hole through the centre of each small shape and eight equally spaced holes in the ring. Wiggle each stick slightly to enlarge the hole but try not to distort the shape. Leave the sticks in place.

3 Return everything to the oven and bake for another twenty minutes in the oven (four minutes in the microwave) then remove the tray and wiggle the sticks up and down again. Repeat this stage once more then remove the sticks and finish the baking. Leave to cool.

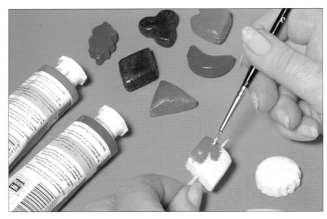

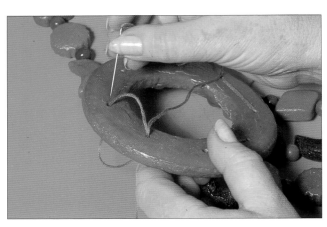

4 Paint one side of the ring and each shape first, leave to dry, then turn over and paint the other side. Apply two or three coats and then two coats of varnish to protect both dough and paint.

5 Cut four 900mm (36in) lengths of silk. Thread two of the ring holes twice to make a double thickness on the top surface. Arrange the hanging pieces so that one is slightly longer than the other.

6 Thread the beads and the shapes alternately, placing four sets on the shorter threads and five sets on the longer ones.

7 Thread a further two beads on each length, double threading the last one and securing the thread with a dab of PVA.

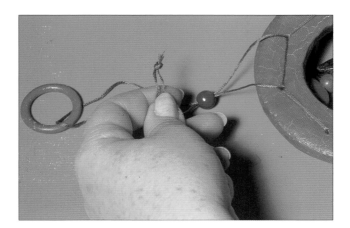

8 Cut four equal lengths of silk. Thread two of the ring holes twice to make a double thickness on the bottom surface of the dough ring. Push both ends of the thread through a bead and one end through the hanging ring then tie a small knot. Arrange the thread so that the knot is half way between the dough ring and the hanging ring, apply a dab of PVA to the knot and then slide the bead up over it. Repeat with the other three lengths of silk.

Salt dough mobile

The finished mobile. You can change the colour scheme and use other shapes to make your mobile. You can also make more intricate shapes by attaching pieces of thinner dough to the main shape with flour paste. This is made by adding enough water to a small piece of dough to give it a cream-like consistency.

Sparkling fish

Long, single mobiles are usually made from brightly contrasting fabrics but, for a change, I thought I would use a single colour and a rich brocade. Soft pastel shades with silver trimming could be used if the mobile is to hang in a baby's room.

The fish template was laid at different angles on the fabric to give various patterns and shades. Individual plastic pearls can be bought from bead shops, or you may find a cheap string at a second-hand shop. The hole in each pearl has to be large enough to accommodate an embroidery silk knot, and the large one (for the hanging thread) must also accept some wire. Try pulling a knot into the hole before starting work on the mobile. If it is too small open it out with your craft knife or a drill.

Tools and materials

Decorative fabric, 75 x 100cm (27 x 36in)

Stiff card, 180mm (7in) square

Black felt-tipped pen

Scissors, craft knife and small pliers

Needle, sewing thread, gold bootlace trimming – about 3m (3yd), embroidery silk

Cotton wool or kapok for stuffing

6 pearls

Self-adhesive holographic paper

160mm (6½in) length of thin brass wire

2m (2yd) florist's ribbon.

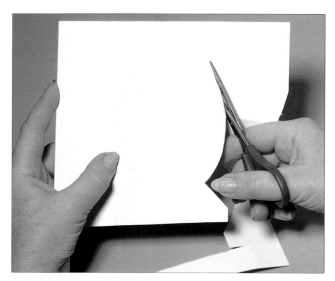

1 Draw a simple fish shape, about 140mm (5½in) long and 85mm (3¼in) wide, on the piece of card. Cut it out with your craft knife or scissors to use as a template.

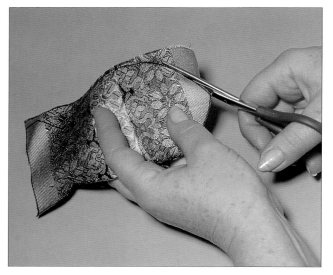

2 Position the template on the fabric, draw round it with a felt pen then cut out the fish shape. Continue until you have twelve fish.

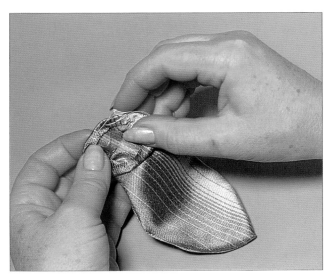

3 Sew two fish, right sides together, leaving the tail end open. Turn the fish inside out and tack down the raw edges of the tail.

4 Push cotton wool into the fish, flattening any lumps, then sew up the tail with small, neat stitches. Remove the tacking.

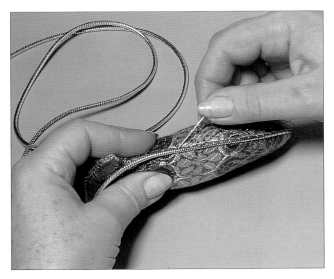

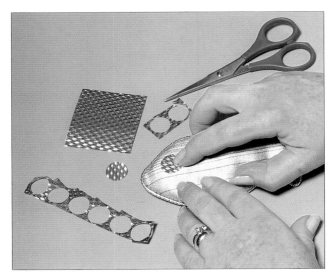

5 Starting at the middle of the tail, sew the trimming round the seam. Use over stitching, which will be hardly noticeable, just catching a little of the fabric at either side of the seam. When almost finished, cut the trimming so that the ends butt up against each other.

6 Cut out twelve 15mm (1/2in) diameter circles of holographic paper and stick one on each side of each fish.

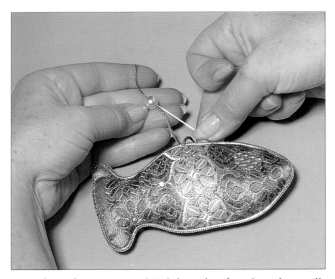

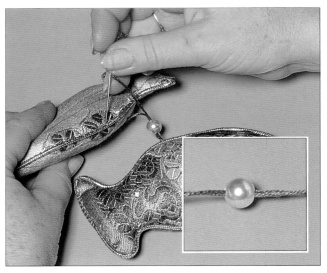

7 Thread a 150mm (6in) length of embroidery silk on to a needle and pass it through a pearl. Push the needle through the top of a fish, at the point where the fish will hang horizontally, then back through the pearl again.

8 Now push the needle through the bottom edge of the next fish. Remove the needle and tie the two ends firmly together. Pull the knot into the middle then slide the pearl up to cover it.

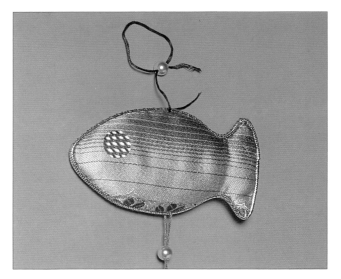

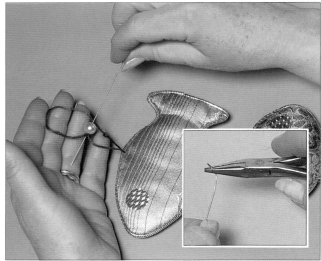

9 Use a 200mm (8in) length of silk for the main hanging thread. Push the needle through the top of the fish, then through the pearl, then round and through the pearl again to form a loop. Remove the needle and tie the two ends firmly together.

10 Push the wire through the pearl, then pull the knot through so that it can't be seen. If necessary adjust the wire so that the pearl is exactly in the middle. Using your pliers carefully bend each end of the wire to form a loop.

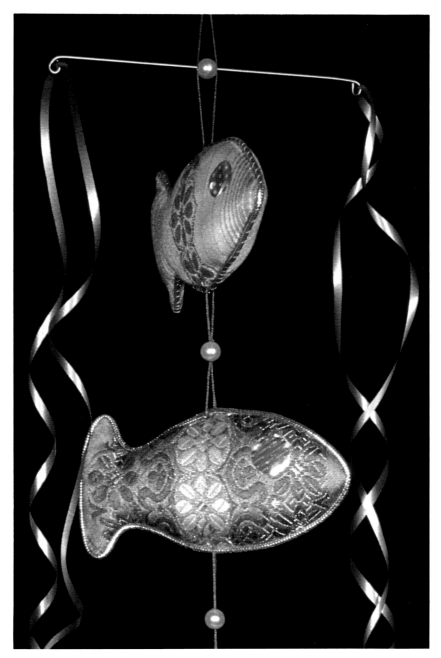

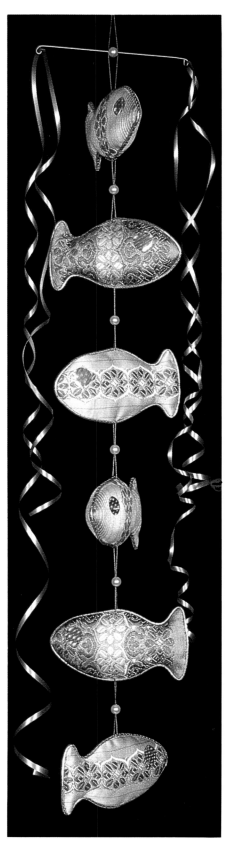

12 Cut two narrow strips from the full length of ribbon. Pull each strip between your thumb and scissor blade; the firmer you pull the tighter the curl will be. Thread each strip through the loops at the end of the wire. More can be added if you like the effect.

Sparkling fish mobile

The finished mobile. Any simplified shape can be used instead of the fish. You could use owls, rabbits or pigs. If you choose pigs, which are always popular, you could give them curled tails made from shorter, thinner lengths of florist's ribbon.

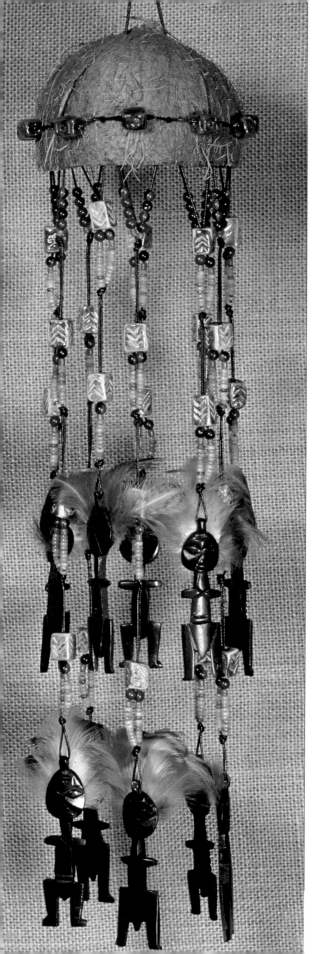

African figures

I bought these little African figures from a bead shop. But, in case you have difficulty finding some, I show you how to make your own from mount board.

The small beads are also available from specialist shops, and I used three types. The smallest range in colour from pale fawn to light brown and orange, the next size are a brighter orange and the larger round ones are swirled with dark brown and black.

I decided to use bootlace thong (a leather-like thread) for hanging the mobile and having already bought my beads, I had to use a drill to open out the holes in the beads.

The larger oblong beads are made from orange and fawn modelling clay which is hardened in the oven. This can be bought from most craft shops. You will need a saw to halve the coconut and a drill to make holes in the shell.

The feathers were plucked from an old feather duster, but small bags of individual feathers can be bought from most craft shops.

Tools and materials

Half a coconut shell

Drill and No.3 drill bit

Tape measure, scrap paper, pencil and a black felt-tipped marker

African figures or, if you make your own:
two pieces of mounting board 200mm (8in) square, black and brown acrylic paint, paint brush, craft knife, steel-edged ruler, cutting mat or thick card, darning needle, 250mm (10in) of uncoated florist's wire, small pliers

Fine bootlace thong – five 660mm (26in) and six 900mm (36in) lengths

Beads – five hundred small ones, sixty slightly larger and ninety larger round ones

Modelling clay – fawn and orange, varnish or clear nail polish burnt umber acrylic paint and a paint brush

Palette knife, kitchen skewer, old ball-point pen

Small feathers – about thirty

Black cartridge paper – 60 x 125mm (2 x 5in), white conté crayon, PVA

1 Measure round the coconut shell with the tape measure then divide the circumference by ten.

2 Mark this number on some paper and mark round the shell 20mm (³⁄₄in) up from the sawn edge.

3 Drill holes through the shell. Drill two more holes through the top for the hanging thread.

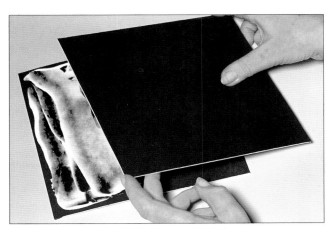

4 Using PVA, stick the two pieces of mounting board together, white side on to black side.

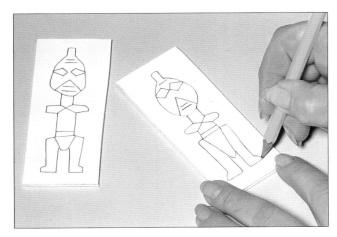

5 Using a craft knife, cut the double-thickness board in half and then cut each half into five rectangles. Draw simple figures on each one.

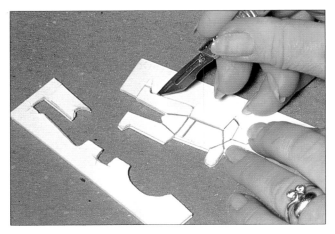

6 Cut out the figures with a craft knife. This will take time, be extra careful as the knife can easily slip.

7 When you have cut out all the figures, change the blade and start to carve the details – angle the blade and slide it along either side of the drawn lines removing V-shaped slivers of card.

8 Put blobs of black and brown acrylic paint on a saucer and paint each figure, using alternate brushfuls of each colour to give a streaky effect. Do not forget to paint the white edges.

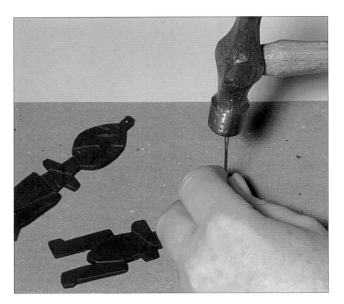

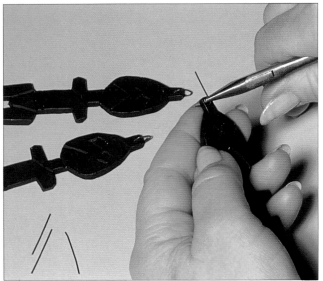

9 Make a hole in the top of each figure with a darning needle. The card is thick so use a hammer or similar to push it through.

10 Using a pair of old scissors cut the wire into ten 25mm (1in) lengths. Insert a piece of wire into the hole and use the pliers to bend it round and form a loop.

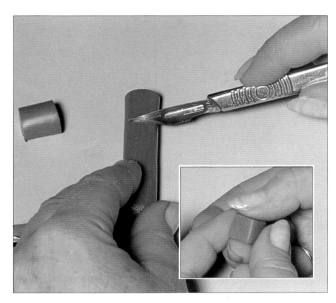

11 Roll the orange modelling clay into a sausage, cut it into ten equal pieces with a craft knife and then model them into 10 x 12mm (³/₈ x ¹/₂in) oblong shapes.

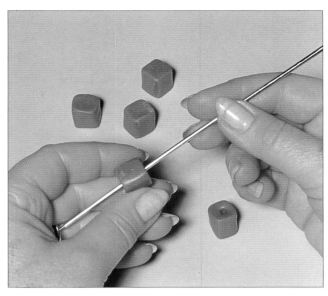

12 Pierce each piece with a skewer, wiggling it to make a hole large enough to accommodate a knotted thong.

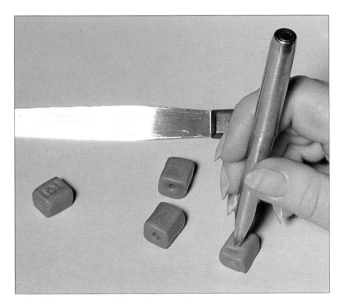

13 Decorate the shapes: I used a palette knife for straight lines and the tip of a spring-loaded, ball-point pen to make small circles. Using fawn clay, make another twenty-five beads, slightly larger in size. Place all the pieces on a oven tray and bake for twenty to thirty minutes at 130°C (265°F) or gas mark 1–2. Allow to cool for ten minutes.

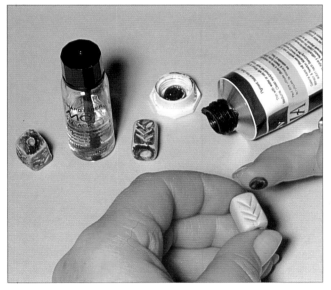

14 Dab your finger inside the lid of a tube of burnt umber acrylic paint then roughly apply paint to the beads leaving the corner edges bare and trying not to get paint into the indentations. The paint will dry almost immediately. Apply a coat of varnish or clear nail polish.

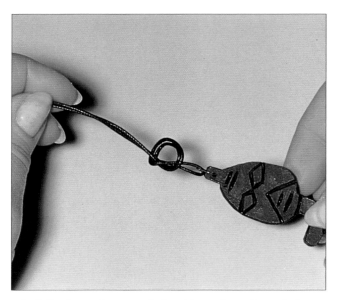

15 Thread one of the short lengths of thong through a wire loop, fold it in half and tie a knot 12mm (½in) up from the head.

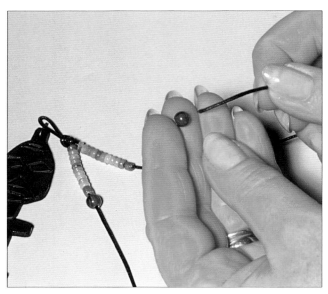

16 Thread ten small beads, one medium-sized one and, finally, one larger round bead on to each piece of thong.

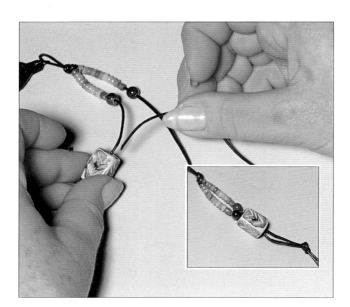

17 Thread both ends of the thong through one of the home-made fawn beads. Tie another knot 40mm (1⅝in) from the fawn bead.

Repeat steps 16 and 17 once more then leave the two ends open. Make up the other four short lengths in the same way.

For the five longer lengths repeat the steps three times ending with a knot. Finally, thread one medium and four round beads on to each of the open ends of thong.

18 Using the white conté crayon draw ten circles (a little smaller than the heads of the figures) on the black cartridge paper and cut them out.

19 Cut three feathers, 60mm (2½in) long, apply a dab of PVA to the back of the head, attach the feathers and leave them to dry.

22 Apply more PVA to one of the black circles and place it neatly over the feathers. Repeat with the remaining figures.

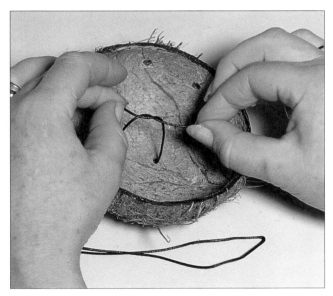

23 Thread the last piece of thong through the holes in the top of the coconut shell. Tie inside with a double knot. Tie another knot about 50mm (2in) above the shell.

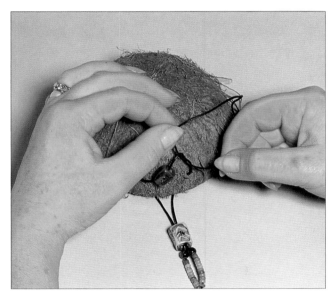

24 Push the two ends of each hanging through two adjacent holes in the shell, from the inside out. Thread a modelled orange bead on to one end then tie the two pieces together, twice. Cut off excess thong then slide the bead over to cover the knot. Repeat with the remaining hangings.

Bouncing clown

Papier mâché is used to make this little fellow. I used wire netting as a former but you can also make up a former from pieces of polystyrene packaging threaded on to lengths of florist's wire.

Wire netting, when cut into small pieces, does have sharp points, so wear gloves when handling it. Use pliers to turn in all sharp points and to manipulate the pieces into shape.

When building up the layers of papier mâché it is easier to use alternate colours so that you can see exactly where the previous layer has been worked. I also used a slightly thicker paper for the final layer.

The mobile is made more interesting for a child by being supported by a spring. I found this spring attached to a cheap key ring which I discarded. If you have difficulty finding a similar one, metal ones are available from craft or hobby shops.

The process of making the mobile is rather involved but well worth the effort and the final model is surprisingly durable.

There are endless possibilities for other models – a couple on a see-saw, a figure on a swing, or a hot-air balloon.

Tools and materials

12mm (½in) wire netting – 300 x 450mm (12 x 18in) or scrap polystyrene packaging and florist's wire

Modelling wire (available from craft shops)

Brass wire – 200mm (8in) length of 2mm (³/₃₂in) and 100mm (4in) length of 1mm (³/₆₄in) (both available from craft shops)

Wire cutters, pliers, pencils, compass, tape measure, darning needle, small pointed scissors, craft knife, drawing pin

Gummed brown-paper parcel tape, small sponge and a dish

Scrap newsprint torn into 20mm (³/₄in) squares, PVA, wallpaper paste, screw-topped jar, mixing and measuring spoons

Round balloon

360mm (14in) length of thread

Water-based white undercoat, various colours of acrylic paint (I used cadmium yellow medium, deep, permanent magenta, titanium white, cadmium red, cerulean blue, permanent deep green and some mixes from these), round and flat paint brushes

Ball of wool (multicoloured if possible), thin card

Coloured paper roughly 50 x 125mm (2 x 5in)

Narrow ribbon – seven 125mm (5in) lengths in different colours

Red modelling clay (which is hardened in the oven) or red plasticine

Small plastic spring

Making papier mâché paste

Mix four tablespoons of wallpaper paste and 300ml (½ pint) of water in a screw-topped jar. Stir rapidly pressing out any lumps. Mix in one tablespoon of PVA. The resulting paste should be thick and smooth, and when left in the screw-topped jar it should last for a few days.

Some wallpaper pastes contain fungicides, so always wash your hands thoroughly when you finish a session of applying papier mâché. Do read the instructions on the packet.

1 Make up a former for the clown: you can thread florist's wire through shaped pieces of polystyrene packaging or you can make it up from pieces of wire netting. The figure is about 300mm (12in) tall.

Wear heavy-duty gloves when handling the wire netting, cut through the single strands of wire and turn the sharp-pointed ends inwards. Thread a piece of modelling wire through the top of the hat and make a loop for hanging the model up to dry.

2 Cut the gummed tape into strips. Wet the strips on the soaked sponge and wrap them tightly and neatly round all parts of the former until it is completely covered.

3 Using the prepared paste, cover the model with overlapping squares of paper, rubbing each piece well down to avoid making creases. Flatten any protruding edges of paper. Wash your hands to remove all traces of paste. Hang up the model to dry; hanging it in an airing cupboard or over a radiator will reduce the drying time to less than an hour.

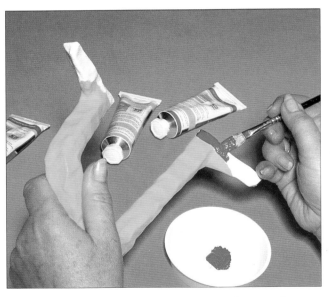

4 Apply another layer of paper squares, allow this layer to dry and then add a final layer of the thicker squares. I find it best to use a different coloured paper for each layer.

5 Apply two coats of water-based white undercoat and then, refering to the picture opposite, paint the clown with acrylic paints.

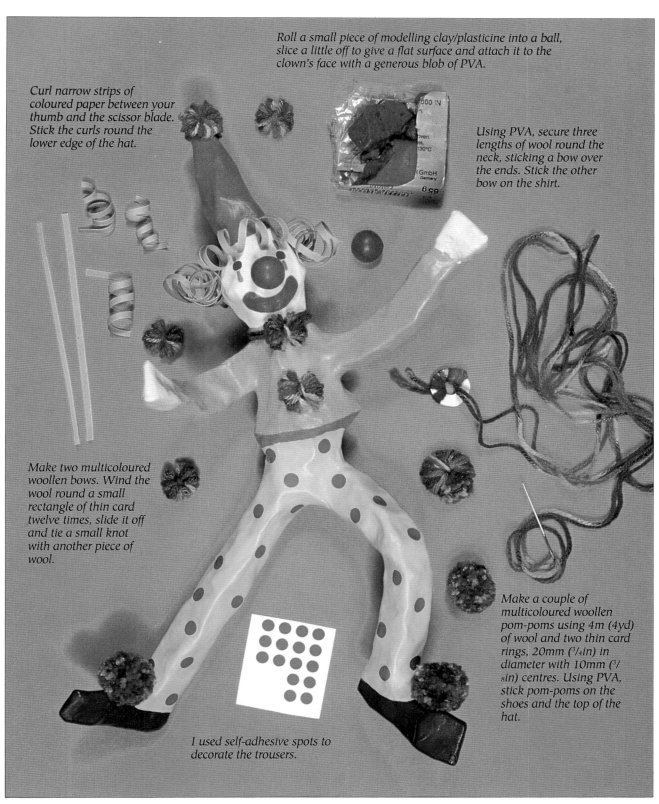

Roll a small piece of modelling clay/plasticine into a ball, slice a little off to give a flat surface and attach it to the clown's face with a generous blob of PVA.

Curl narrow strips of coloured paper between your thumb and the scissor blade. Stick the curls round the lower edge of the hat.

Using PVA, secure three lengths of wool round the neck, sticking a bow over the ends. Stick the other bow on the shirt.

Make two multicoloured woollen bows. Wind the wool round a small rectangle of thin card twelve times, slide it off and tie a small knot with another piece of wool.

Make a couple of multicoloured woollen pom-poms using 4m (4yd) of wool and two thin card rings, 20mm (^{3}/$_4$in) in diameter with 10mm (^{3}/$_8$in) centres. Using PVA, stick pom-poms on the shoes and the top of the hat.

I used self-adhesive spots to decorate the trousers.

6 Decorate the clown: use the accessories shown above or experiment with your own ideas.

Bouncing clown mobile

7 Blow up the balloon, not too big, and cover roughly two thirds of it with three layers of paper and a coat of PVA to form the umbrella. Apply another layer of newsprint, a final layer of the thicker paper and a further coat of PVA.

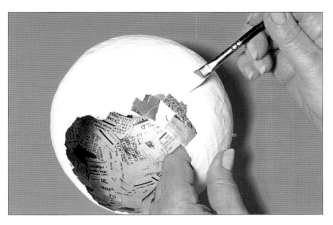

8 When the PVA is dry burst the balloon, and paint the rough umbrella shape with two coats of white undercoat.

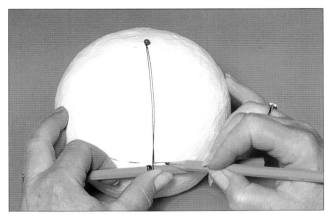

9 Fix a length of thread to a drawing pin pushed into the top of the umbrella shape. Attach a pencil to the end of the thread, 100mm (4in) from the pin hole, and draw a circumference line with another pencil.

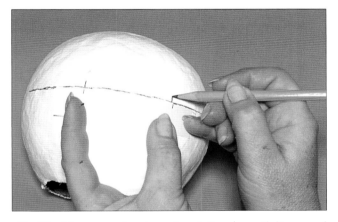

10 Measure the length of the pencil line and divide the number by seven. Mark this measurement on a strip of paper, take it round the circumference line to divide it into seven segments.

11 Lay the tape measure from the pin hole at the top of the umbrella shape down to each point on the circumference line and, using the tape as a guide, draw a line.

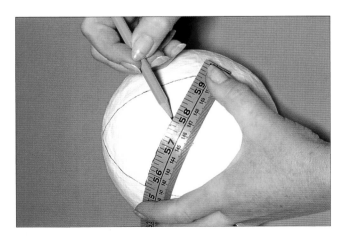

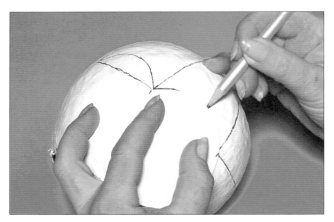

12 Cut an 80mm (3¼in) circle from a piece of scrap paper. Position it over the circumference line touching two of the points and draw an arc. Continue until all the seven arcs have been drawn.

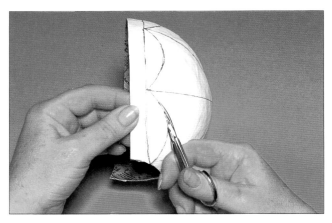

13 Cut round the shape close to the circumference line, then cut away the curved areas using curved scissors if you have them.

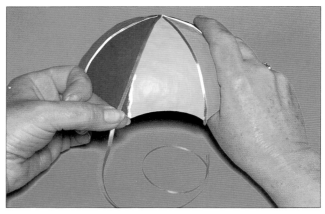

14 Leaving the pin in the hole so that it does not get blocked, paint and PVA the umbrella. When it is dry, apply PVA down the seams and stick down pieces of ribbon. Cut the ends of the ribbon to neat points.

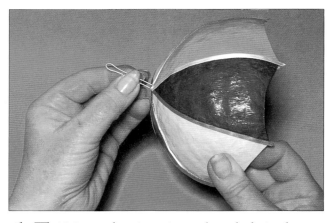

15 Using a drawing pin, make a hole in the top of the umbrella close to the original one. Bend the fine brass wire in half and push the two ends through the two holes.

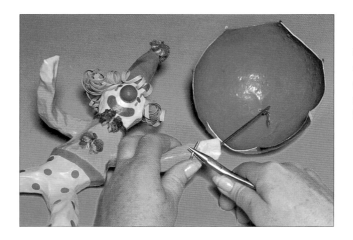

16 Using pliers, make a closed loop at one end of the thick brass wire then thread one of the ends of fine wire through the closed loop and twist the ends tightly together. Carefully manipulate the other end of the thick wire round the clown's wrist. Finally, attach your spring to the fine wire loop and the mobile is now ready to bounce.

Making mobiles from natural materials

CHINESE LANTERNS • LAMINATED AUTUMN LEAVES

TEASEL FLOWERS • TWIRLING SEEDS

DRIED SUMMER FLOWERS • CHRISTMAS TREE

Chinese Lanterns

As my husband is a gardener we are often given bags of tomatoes or apples, seeds, cuttings or uncommon plants, by some of his generous customers. Last autumn he came home with a bucket full of Chinese lanterns *(Physalis franchetii)*, which were just begging to be arranged in some unusual way. I selected six stems, removed their leaves and tied them together. Some of the remaining lanterns were a more vivid orange so, to add more interest, I cut them off and hung them from the stems with threaded melon seeds. (Chinese lanterns will grow in any soil but you should position them in a corner of the garden away from other plants as their roots are invasive. They thrive in full sun or partial shade.)

Tools and materials

Several Chinese lantern stems and some melon seeds (see the notes below about cutting and drying them)

Sticky tape and strong clear glue

String

Sturdy cardboard tube (I used one from a roll of kitchen wrap)

Craft knife or junior hack-saw and a pair of scissors

Acrylic paints – I used cadmium red and cadmium yellow – and a paint brush

Invisible nylon thread and a long darning needle

Drying the lanterns and seeds

Cut some stems from the plant when the lanterns are a delicate, pale orange and the stems are still green and pliable. Place them in a dry bucket or vase where they will automatically bend over. Leave them to dry out completely for about two weeks. The lanterns will become a deeper shade of orange the longer they are left on the plant, so only cut these off when they have reached maturity.

Wash the melon seeds thoroughly. Pat them in a tea towel, then leave to dry spread on a piece of kitchen paper in the airing cupboard, or another warm place, for three or four days.

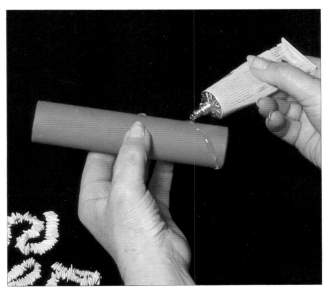

1 Cut five or six dried stems to an appropriate length and then tie a generous length of string round the stems, making a loop at the top for hanging.

2 Cut the cardboard tube to cover the length of the tied stems and apply three coats of paint. Using invisible thread and the darning needle make two lengths of melon seeds. Apply two spirals of glue up the length of the tube.

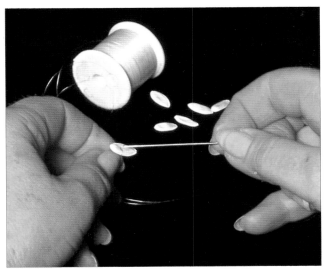

3 Stick the lengths of threaded seeds on to the spirals of glue, making sure the seeds are all laying the same way.

4 Thread the needle with more invisible thread and secure a small seed on the end, knotting the thread twice.

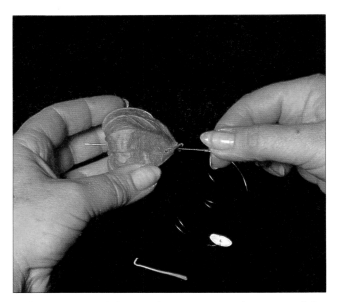

5 Cut the stalk from a lantern, open the point of the lantern, insert the needle, push it through the back and pull the seed into the lantern.

6 Thread thirty to forty seeds behind the lantern.

7 Attach the seeds and lantern to one of the stems, sewing into the stem then winding the thread round twice. Tie a neat knot to finish. Continue to attach more lanterns until you are happy with the arrangement.

The Chinese lantern mobile

Autumn leaves mobile

Other versions of this very pretty mobile can be decorated with brightly coloured berries or the seeds from the same trees as the leaves.

Autumn leaves

I had intended this mobile to be full of berries, seeds, dried flower heads and other lovely things found in the woods and hedgerows during the autumn months. However, these leaves looked so pretty, with the light of a window or lamp coming through them from behind, that anything else detracted from their simple beauty.

In order to protect the leaves, which become rather brittle after drying and pressing, I encased each between two pieces of clear acetate, using a strong clear glue to hold everything together. The leaves then looked as if they had been trapped in a sheet of winter ice.

Leaves can be pressed at any time of the year, but autumn produces the greatest range of colours – from subtle greens and greys through to rich browns and reds. Gather a variety of leaves: look for interesting shapes, different sizes and, of course, lots of colours. Place them between several sheets of newspaper and cover with a flat, heavy weight. Check them occasionally – they should be ready to use after about three weeks.

Tools and materials

An interesting branch stripped of leaves

Pressed autumn leaves

Sheets of clear acetate (available from art and craft shops), clear, strong adhesive and a palette knife

Scissors, craft knife and a cutting mat (or a sheet of thick card)

Scrap paper (for use when applying glue)

Needle, invisible nylon thread and some brown embroidery silk for hanging the mobile.

1 Place one sheet of acetate exactly on top of another. Arrange several leaves on top with generous margins around each. Pressing firmly down and remembering the margin, cut round each leaf with your craft knife.

Lay each leaf and its two shapes of acetate on a piece of scrap paper side by side. Work as quickly and carefully as possible through the next stages because the glue is fast-drying.

2 Apply zigzags of glue to each piece of acetate then quickly spread it with your palette knife to cover the whole surface.

3 Position the leaf, leaving an equal border all round, and cover with the other sheet of acetate. Press firmly to squeeze out excess glue. Repeat until all the leaves are encased.

4 When the glue has set, trim round each leaf leaving a border of about 3mm (1/8in).

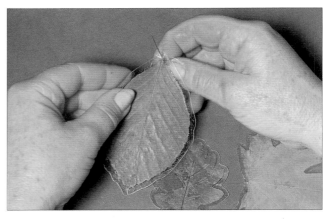

5 Cut several lengths of thread and sew rows of leaves together, at different angles, leaving gaps so that the leaves can twist and turn. Leave enough thread at the end to tie round the branch.

6 Make a neat loop at one end of the embroidery silk. Tie the other end securely round a thick part of the branch, which should hang more or less horizontally. If possible, hang the branch up temporarily and study its form to get an idea of where best to position each row of leaves. When this has been decided carefully make small diagonal cuts in the branches and slot in the rows of leaves.

Teasel flowers

The dried flower heads of sea holly (*Eryngium spp*) are known as teasels. The stems are covered with fine thorns so you may wish to wear gloves when sorting out the heads. The leaves for this mobile were pressed as described on page 47. Choose lobed leaves – maple, sycamore, London plane – to give interest to the final shape. The completed teasel flowers are pushed on to lengths of brass wire.

Tools and materials

Teasels (twelve of various sizes, but not too large)

Pressed leaves (thirty-six all about the same size)

Scissors, small pliers and a craft knife

PVA, paint brush and scrap paper

Double-sided sticky tape and clear sticky tape

Uncoated florist's wire and twelve 300mm (12in) lengths of 1mm brass wire

Darning needle, length of embroidery silk.

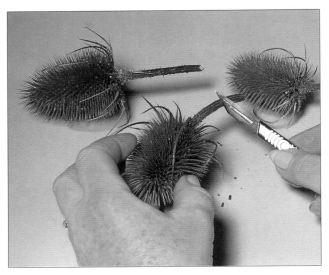

1 Cut off the teasel heads leaving a 50mm (2in) stem. Gently tap each head on to scrap paper to remove the seeds. Hold the end of the stem over a piece of paper and use your craft knife (scraping towards the head) to remove the thorns.

2 Place the leaves vein side down on a table and, using narrow strips of sticky tape, fix a length of florist's wire on the front of each leaf. Cut the wire to leave a 50mm (2in) stalk.

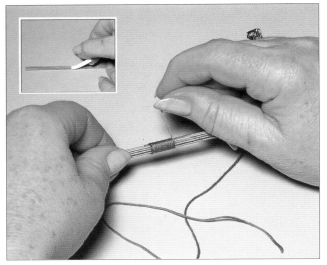

3 Mix some PVA with a little water in a dish or small screw-topped jar. Place each leaf on a piece of scrap paper and paint one side completely (it will dry clear and protect the leaf by making it less brittle). Allow the leaves to dry for about four hours then paint the other sides.

4 While the leaves are drying prepare the hanging wires. Arrange the wires as a block of three rows of four wires. Use narrow strips of double-sided sticky tape to hold the layers together. Take another strip of the tape and stick it round all the wires, about 50mm (2in) from one end. Stick the end of a length of embroidery silk on to the tape and bind it neatly round to cover the tape.

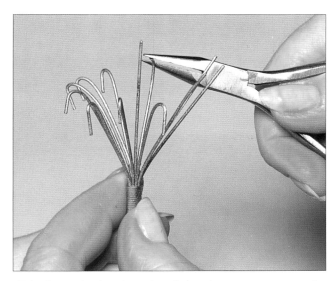

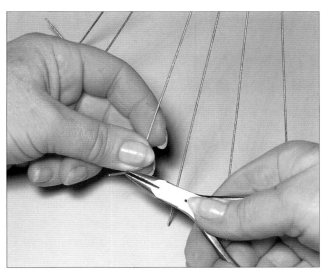

5 Above the binding, bend the short wires outwards, leaving the centre one straight. Using your pliers, curl the ends round. Make a tighter curl on the centre wire for the hanging thread. Double a piece of silk, knot it neatly and thread it through the centre wire.

6 Now bend out the long lengths of wires just below the binding. Using the pliers, turn up the last 20mm (³⁄₄in) of each wire to form an angle of 45°, facing outwards.

7 When the leaves have dried, carefully wrap the wire stems of three of them round the stem of each teasel, keeping the wires pushed as close to the teasel head as possible. If the wire wraps round more than three times, cut the excess off (the thickness of stems will vary).

8 Cut the stems to 20mm (³⁄₄in). Push the darning needle as far as it will go into each stem, pull it out, then carefully push the flower teasels on to the angled wires.

Finally, adjust the wires so that the teasel flowers lie together, side by side, in the form of a ring. The mobile is now ready to hang.

Twirling seeds

Who could resist the fluttering, twirling seeds of the maple and sycamore trees? These were gathered early one misty autumn morning when I was cycling through our local park. The larger maple seeds were pressed between sheets of newspaper with a couple of heavy books on top. The rows at the top of the mobile are pumpkin seeds – which we sprinkle on our breakfast cereal each morning and which can be bought at most health-food stores.

Tools and materials

Large and medium maple seeds, several small bunches of sycamore seeds and approximately 80g (3oz) of pumpkin seeds

Wire ring 350mm (14in) diameter (available from most craft shops)

Florist's green tape (available from florists and craft shops)

Green mounting board, 300 x 380mm (12 x 15in)

Scissors, pencil, ruler and an emery board

Green acrylic paint, roughly the same colour as the mounting board, and a paint brush

Strong clear glue, PVA and masking tape

Green embroidery silk

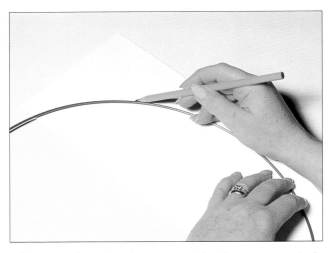

1 Using the wire ring as a guide, draw a part circle with a depth of 125mm (5in) at its widest point on the white side of the board.

2 Cut the shape out as smoothly as possible along the pencil line. Use this shape as a template to make a second one. Smooth the curved edges with the emery board.

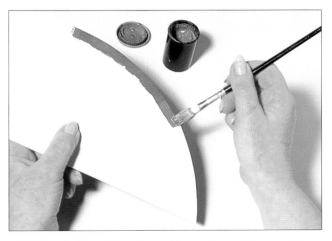

3 Carefully paint the white edges, then paint a border about 25mm (1in) wide round the edge of each white side.

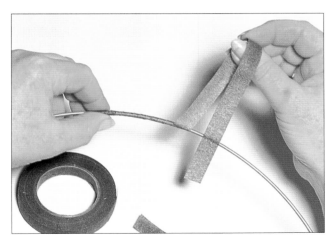

4 Cut strips of florist's tape into 300mm (12in) lengths and wrap it round the ring (it sticks to itself) until the ring is completely covered.

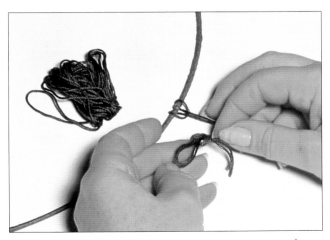

5 Cut a length of embroidery silk, fold it in half and tie it to the ring as the hanging thread.

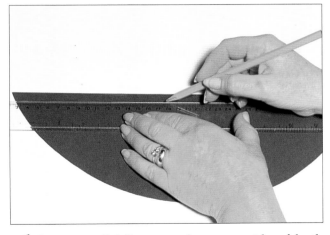

6 Draw parallel lines on the green side of both pieces of card, roughly 10mm (3/8in) apart.

7 Apply a line of clear glue on the back of one card, slightly in from the curved edge. Ensure that the hanging thread is at an angle and place the ring on the card. Place a heavy book, or similar weight, on top until the glue has dried.

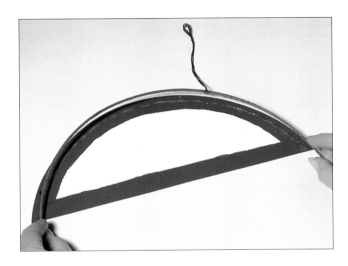

8 Split a length of silk into separate strands. Select five or six bunches of sycamore seeds and tie a strand to each. Position the bunches of seeds on to the card and secure with neat pieces of masking tape.

9 Turn the mobile over and stick rows of pumpkin seeds along the pencil lines with tiny blobs of PVA. When these rows are complete, attach the other piece of card to the ring as step 7, and stick rows of seeds to that side.

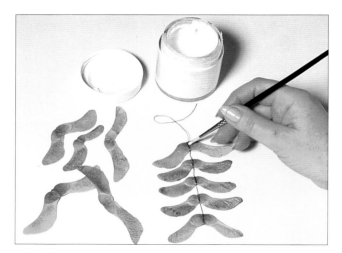

10 Split another length of silk into strands. Choose any number of the pressed maple seeds and arrange them in three rows. Apply a little PVA to the centre of the first seed then wrap the thread round twice. Leave a gap (about 20mm (³/₄in) for larger seeds and 10mm (³/₈in) for medium seeds) then stick the next seed to the thread. Continue until you have three attached rows of seeds.

11 Tie each row of seeds round the ring using dabs of PVA to secure.

Twirling seeds mobile

The finished mobile made from maple, sycamore and pumpkin seeds. If you look around, I am sure you will find lots of other types of seed that can be used.

Summer flowers

Any pressed flowers can be used for this mobile. I chose Geraniums because we had a profusion of them in our kitchen window box, and borage flowers because they are smaller (necessary for the cut-outs) and so pretty. The petals can be pressed between a couple of nappy liners and several thicknesses of newspaper, with a heavy weight placed on top. It takes about six weeks for them to dry out completely, after which they are rather delicate so handle them with care. The ivy leaves (which are much tougher) were pressed in the same way.

Tools and materials

Wire ring 180mm (7in) diameter (available from most craft shops) and green florist's tape (available from florists or craft shops)

Green embroidery silk and some string or fine wool

Pressed flower petals and leaves

Four A4 (8 x 12in) sheets of thin, pale green card, three A4 (8 x 12in) sheets of clear acetate and three A3 (12 x 16in) sheets of dry adhesive (both available from graphic design suppliers and some art and craft shops)

Double-sided sticky tape and PVA

Green acrylic paint and a paint brush

Invisible nylon thread

Sharp pointed scissors

Scrap paper

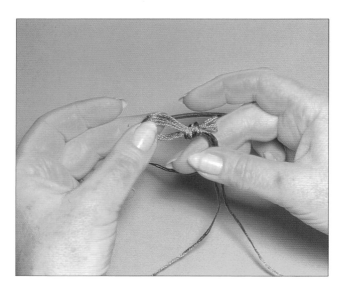

1 Cover the ring with florist's tape, as described on page 53. Cut four lengths of the green silk or string. Fold them in half and thread each on to the ring at equal intervals. Pull the lengths up and tie together forming a neat hanging loop.

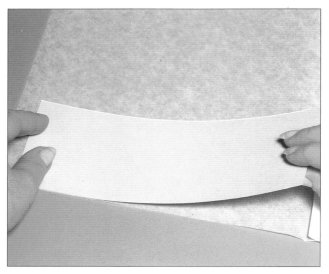

2 Cut each piece of card and acetate into three (this size is more manageable). Lay a piece of card on to the dry adhesive, press the entire surface firmly, then lift it off.

3 Arrange the petals on to the glued card to form simple flowers leaving a cutting space between each. Press the petals down lightly.

4 When the card is full, lay a piece of acetate on to the dry adhesive. Apply pressure, lift, then carefully press on to the arranged petals.

5 Cut the flowers out leaving a neat, narrow border round each.

6 Lay four flower shapes face down. Attach a piece of double-sided tape to each and press a length of invisible thread across them all.

7 Attach pieces of double-sided tape to the back of four smaller cut-outs then stick these on to the centre of the larger ones. Press them down firmly.

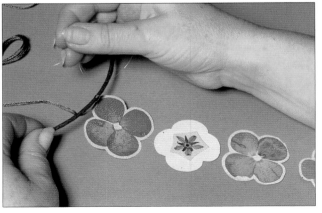

8 Tie the strands of petals at equal distances round the ring.

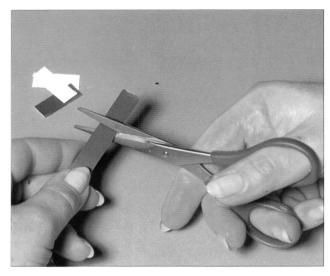

9 Apply two coats of green paint to one side of three of the pieces of card. When the paint is dry, cover the back of one of the painted cards with double-sided sticky tape and then cut it into small pieces, about 25 x 10mm (1 x ³⁄₈in). These will be used to attach the leaves to the ring.

10 Choose about twelve leaves of various shapes and colours. Apply PVA to the back of the leaves and stick them to the back of the other two painted cards. Leave a gap between each leaf to allow for cutting. When the glue has dried, carefully cut out the leaves with a narrow border round each.

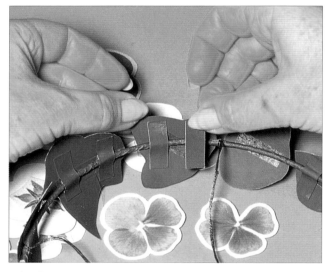

11 Decide on the angle at which you want the leaf to be positioned on the ring. Attach a neat piece of double-sided sticky tape on to the back (painted side) of the leaf and position it on the ring.

12 Remove the backing from the double-side tape on one or two pieces of green card (the number used depends on the size of the leaf) and stick these over the ring and on to the back of the leaf. Continue until the ring is complete.

Summer flowers mobile

I used eight sets of geranium flowers for this mobile, but you can use more or less, depending on the size of your chosen flowers.

Christmas tree

The foliage for this Christmas decoration is Leyland Cypress *(Cupressocyparis leylandii)*, which was pressed for about five weeks before assembling the mobile, as described on page 47. Any similar foliage can be used, the variegated variety would look particularly good. The trunk of the tree is made from pressed beech leaves, cut into strips and stuck on to the card frame. The pine cones can be found in autumn, strewn over the ground of some woodland areas. They can also be bought from craft shops or florists.

Tools and materials

Fir cones (nine, roughly the same size)

Lots of pressed cypress foliage

Large, pressed beech leaves

4B and HB pencils, steel-edged ruler

A2 (16 x 24in) sheet of 5mm (¼in) graph paper

Green mounting board – two A2 (16 x 24in) sheets

Craft knife, cutting mat (or thick cardboard) and a pair of scissors

Green acrylic paint (similar colour to the mounting board) and a small flat paint brush

Invisible nylon thread (for hanging the cones)

Green embroidery silk (for hanging the mobile), a darning and an embroidery needle

PVA, double-sided sticky tape and masking tape

Rough shape of the Christmas tree used for this mobile. If you are worried about drawing angles, you could make the tree a simple triangle with straight sides.

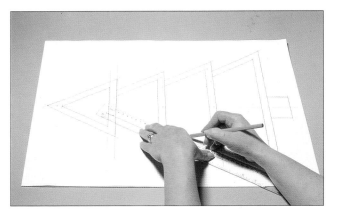

1 The size of your cones will determine the size of the tree so, first arrange the cones on a sheet of paper then roughly draw the tree round them, leaving space for the cones to swing a little.

Now draw a more accurate plan on the graph paper using the 4B pencil; press firmly so you can see the lines through the back. Make each section of frame at least 20mm (¾in) wide. Mark dots for the cone threads and one more for the hanging thread. Draw a trunk 50mm (2in) deep and 75mm (3in) wide.

3 Turn the paper over and attach it, with masking tape, to the white side of one of the boards. Trace the frame and dots using your HB pencil. Repeat with the second sheet of board, this time omitting the dots.

4 Using your ruler and craft knife cut out the centre pieces of tree first, then the remainder. Using this shape as a template, cut out another frame from the second piece of card.

5 Push a darning needle through the pencil dots. It is easier to drive the needle through by tapping it with a small hammer.

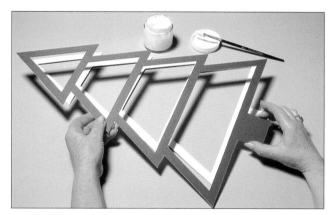

6 Apply a coat of PVA to the white side of one tree, then stick the two together. Push the holes made in step 5 through the second sheet.

7 Paint all the white edges green.

8 Thread a needle with a double length of silk. Knot it and pass it through the top hole twice to form the hanging loop.

9 Cut a 350mm (14in) length of invisible thread and thread both ends through the embroidery needle. Wrap the thread twice round the central sprig of the cone, pass the needle through the loop and pull the thread taut.

10 Pass the thread through a hole and round the bar three times. Secure it with small pieces of double-sided sticky tape on both sides. Cut off excess thread but do not remove the backing from the tape at this stage.

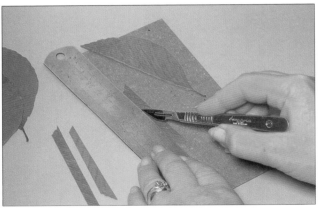

11 Using a craft knife, cut out the thick central vein and stem, then cut the leaf into neat strips. Use the reverse side of some to vary the colour.

12 Carefully attach the strips with PVA . Turn the tree over and trim off excess leaf. Repeat the above on this side of the trunk.

13 Using generous blobs of PVA on the stems, stick on the foliage. Start at the bottom and work from right to left, with the stem pointing left. Each piece should overlap the previous one, covering all the glue. Occasionally check that the foliage does not prevent the cones from swinging. Next, work the two sides of the lowest tier, starting at the bottom with stems pointing upwards. Work the next horizontal from left to right. Continue up the tree alternating the direction of the horizontals. Allow the top to dry for a few minutes then carefully turn the tree over and cover the other side in the same way.

Christmas tree mobile

This mobile uses natural cones, but there is no reason why they should not be sprayed silver or gold. The tree could also be decorated with tiny metallic balls.

Index